P9-APW-615

Angels and Men

Angels and Men

Ladislaus Boros

Illustrated by

Max von Moos

Translated by
John Maxwell

UNITY SCHOOL LIBRARY
UNITY VILLAGE DISCARD 64065

A Crossroad Book
THE SEABURY PRESS • NEW YORK

1977
The Seabury Press
815 Second Avenue
New York, N.Y. 10017

All rights reserved. No part of this book may be repro-
duced, stored in a retrieval system, or transmitted, in any
form or by any means, electronic, mechanical, photocopy-
ing, recording or otherwise, without the written permission
of The Seabury Press.

Originally published as
Engel und Menschen
© Walter Verlag AG Olten 1974
Illustrations © Max von Moos

This Translation and arrangement
© Search Press Ltd 1976

Library of Congress Catalog Card Number: 77-71711
ISBN: 0-8164-0329-5
Printed in the United States of America

Contents

Foreword

I planned this book together with Max von Moos. It is not a 'treatise' on the angels. There are enough historical and theological books of angelology. This one is much more modest in scope. I wanted to readjust people's thinking to the presence of those beings who, whether good or evil, are 'superior' to us and often play a part in our destiny. I have tried to help people to tune in to the angels once again.

Unfortunately, present-day Christians would rather not talk about them. Yet they have an essential part to play in Christian faith.

I have tried to make these meditations as short as the subject demands, and to use them to prompt the right kind of awareness of angels. I have avoided footnotes; they would only distract the reader. The quotations (other than those from the Bible) do not need scholarly verification. And the book is often intentionally incomplete; what I really want to do is to start a train of thought.

I have posed a major problem in this book, or, rather, I have suggested an 'alternative'. We must not leave the angels to fanatics who would exaggerate their significance. Yet it is pointless to discuss them in abstract theological terms. Both approaches are excessive or easily lead to superficial and fanciful speculation (that does not mean, of course, that theologians should ignore the angels).

This book isn't, I suppose, quite in line with the 'modern thought' that is still fashionable. It takes some courage to write about angels nowadays, especially when the intention is not to complete a comprehensive thesis, but to make an honest attempt at helping the reader to sense their immediate presence. Throughout this book I am concerned to defend only one hypothesis (often only implying or intimating my point, in order to avoid awakening rancour): The angels help us to understand Jesus. The angels are pointers to Jesus, or signs of Christ and his works. In his death and resurrection Jesus Christ defeated all the powers. And so Jesus became our only angel.

I hope that this book will please my readers as well as those who warm to Max von Moos's pictures. Max von Moos and I belong to rather different 'camps'. Only our friendship, despite all disagreements and differences, made this joint work possible. Perhaps we contradict one another. Perhaps the text doesn't fit the pictures here and there, or the other way round. But I hope that we show that we agree on essentials. Even if we do not, that too can be of help.

Ladislaus Boros

Appearing angels

Appearing angels

The best place to begin is where we see the angels most closely –
when they appear to men. According to the scriptural reports of
angelic visitations, angels have appeared quite often. I want to look
at three of them closely. They are in the three visions of St Joseph.
All we know of them is a few sentences in the gospels of Luke and
Matthew. Not a word that Joseph said has been handed down to us.
Clearly he didn't say a lot. He is impressive for a different reason:
because he obeyed. We don't even know if Joseph was still alive
when Jesus began to reveal himself to people as the Messiah. Yet
the silence of the Gospel speaks louder than any words.

Joseph's life was self-effacement. He was unassuming. Nothing
shocked or enraged him. His faith and trust make him an ideal
figure for us to follow. He lived a very secluded life with the wife
he loved. Throughout his life he trusted in something incredible.
He stayed in that obscurity for a long time – a lifetime. His hands
were empty. God tested his earthly love; and he was silent. In the
end all that was left for him was to die, taking his earthly despair
with him into the impenetrable: there to be a love that craves and
longs no more. Joseph always bowed to the incomprehensible.

11

Three times an angel
appeared to Joseph in his sleep

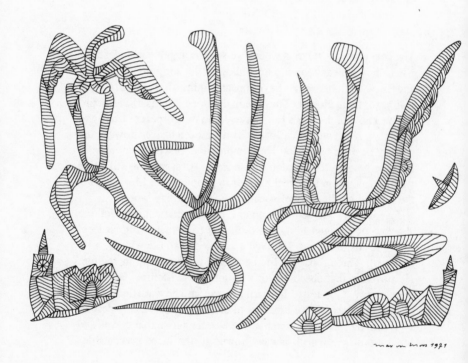

Perhaps, deep down inside, he was puzzled and disconcerted. An angel appeared to him. Each appearance was a command.

First: 'An angel of the Lord appeared to him in a dream. "Joseph son of David", said the angel, "do not be afraid to take Mary home with you as your wife. It is by the Holy Spirit that she has conceived this child"' (Mt 1.20). We can only guess what that meant for Joseph. He had loved Mary. And no one, not even God, can tear someone we love from our heart. Yet now he found – indeed, being a man, he must have found – that his wife had been unfaithful to him. Inwardly this quiet man was very much a man of principle. He silently resolved to leave Mary. As he thought the problem over that night, God came to his aid. He did so through a 'mediator' – an angel. In the harshness and anguish of fate, human existence moves to the very boundaries of the world; but there, at the edge of things, we can glimpse the meaning of life.

A messenger of the Lord 'appeared' to Joseph as he thought things over in the darkness of night, and brought him *help*. This was no superficial aid but something which revealed to him the mystery of the Incarnation – of God's becoming man. We have to try to realize that here dishonour was very close to the sacred. Sometimes it is very difficult to understand that in our lives. Joseph believed in Mary's holiness, but it was still a mystery for him. That is one of the most important functions of angels in our lives: they bring us help in a situation from which there seems to be no way out. If we have to help others in the same way, we do at least a part of the angel's work. Then, for our fellow men, we are like angels. We don't replace the angels, but make it possible for our neighbours to get closer to God. Then we become *angeloi* – God's ambassadors and messengers – for our neighbours.

Second: 'An angel of the Lord appeared to Joseph in a dream, and said to him, "Rise up, take the child and his mother and escape with them to Egypt, and stay there until I tell you"' (Mt 2.13). In this vision the angel appeared as a *saviour* in a situation of need. Not of course *the* Saviour, who is always God himself, but as an ambassador of salvation. That is an essential function of angels. For us God is always the one who saves. But he is so good that he does not intervene directly in each and every case, but gives his creatures the opportunity to act.

I should be very pleased if we Christians could stop talking about a God of retribution and punishment. Our God is a Lord full of mercy; he is long-suffering and rich in loving-kindness. I know that in the past we held up another 'image of God' before people. But fundamentally our God is a God of salvation. He does not want to leave us in a state of despair. And so he sent us his messengers of salvation, in order to free us from need. I must also add that when we are in a position to help others or even just one other in need, then we are already God's messengers.

Third: 'The time came that Herod died; and an angel of the Lord appeared in a dream to Joseph in Egypt and said to him, "Rise up, take the child and his mother, and go with them to the land of Israel"' (Mt 2.19–20). In this angelic visitation there was an unmistakable *task* for Joseph. When an angel 'appears' to us, there is always a commission. At the end of the account of Jesus' temptation, we read: 'Then the devil left him; and angels appeared and waited on him' (Mt 4.11). This service by the angels meant work for Jesus too: 'From that day Jesus began to proclaim the message: "Repent for the kingdom of Heaven is upon you"' (Mt 4.17). I must stress again that when we undertake a commission for our neighbours, we should not feel ashamed. We have to make it possible for them really to fulfil the task in question. Then we shall have performed a part at least of the messenger-task of the angels in our own lives.

I am trying, bit by bit, to piece together what the image of an angel means for us men. Until now I have mentioned only angelic appearances in the past. But the significance for our own lives is what I want to stress: being a help to our neighbour, standing by him in need and passing on a task to him; those are our angelic deeds. Human existence is also being sent from God to men. Life is a form of angelic service.

Accompanying angels

Accompanying angels

The Book of Tobit tells one of the most gripping stories in the Old Testament – indeed in world literature as a whole. Old Tobit, who lives a life of principle in accordance with the law of Israel, is taken captive and deported to Nineveh where he meets with various misfortunes and finally blindness. At the same time Raguel, a relative, is living in Media. Raguel has a daughter called Sarah. The poor girl is pursued by bad luck. She was betrothed to seven men, but they were all killed on the marriage night. Even her maidservant jeers at her because of that. The fates of Tobit and Sarah seem sealed. They are people without a future. But Tobit remembers that he has lent some money to another kinsman, Gabael of Rages in Media. So he sends his son Tobias to fetch the money he deposited, before he, Tobit, dies. But Tobias doesn't know how to get to Media and looks for someone to go with him. And here the story proper begins.

'Tobias went out to find a man who knew the way and would accompany him to Media, and found himself face to face with the angel Raphael. Not knowing he was an angel of God he questioned him ...' (Tob 5.4). This is an important sign. God's messenger can appear in our lives without our being aware of it. Like Jesus himself, the Son of God, who was put in a crib and later became a carpenter.

'The boy and the angel left the house together, and the dog came out with him and accompanied them' (Tob 6.2). Just a small detail; one perhaps that raises a smile.

All three, man, angel and beast, are God's creatures, and belong together. Suddenly there is an accident. Tobias wants to bathe his feet in the river but a huge fish jumps out of the water and tries to swallow the boy's foot. Tobias seizes the fish and refuses to let go. The angel tells Tobias to split the fish open and take out its gall, heart and liver. He is to use the heart and liver as a fumigation in front of anyone plagued by an evil demon. The gall is for use as an eye ointment.

They go on their way to Media. When they get there the angel gives Tobias some good advice. He is to marry Sarah, for he is her next of kin and has a right to Sarah's hand. 'Raphael said to him . . . "When you enter the bridal chamber, take some of the fish's liver and its heart, and put them on the smoking incense. The smell will spread, and when the demon smells it he will make off and never be seen near her any more. When you are about to go to bed with her, both of you must first stand up and pray, beseeching the Lord of heaven to grant you mercy and deliverance"' (Tob 6.16–18).

That seems to me another very significant event. The angel concerns himself with purely 'earthly things', such as the happiness of two human beings. Angels aren't anti-world. They probably understand our worries better than we do.

Then comes the marriage feast. Tobias does as the angel says. Tobias and Sarah pray before they get into bed. Raphael follows the demon and binds him hand and foot (Tob 8.3).

But 'Raguel got up and summoned his servants, and they went out and dug a grave' (Tob 8.9). He thinks that Tobias has been killed like his predecessors. They send the maidservant into the bedroom to see what has happened. What a surprise. There they are, sleeping peacefully. 'She came out and told them: "He is alive and has come to no harm"' (Tob 8.14). The next day Tobias calls the angel Raphael and says '. . . my friend, take four servants with

Love
cancels
danger

you, and two camels, and make your way to Rages. Go to Gabael's house, give him the bond and collect the money, and bring him with you to the wedding-feast' (Tob 9.2).

Gabael comes. He blesses Tobias and his wife. They celebrate the wedding-feast. 'Raguel handed over to Tobias Sarah his bride and half of all that he possessed, male and female slaves, sheep and cattle, donkeys and camels, clothes, money, and furniture. He saw them safely off and embraced Tobias' (Tob 10.10–11). 'Raphael said, "You know how your father was when we left him; let us hurry on ahead of your wife and see that the house is ready before the others arrive"' (Tob 11.1–3). The angel is ready to serve men. An angel doesn't overwhelm us with his presence. He just keeps near us, giving advice, guiding and leading us. Something really outstanding is never blatant or presumptuous.

Finally the two arrive at old Tobit's house. 'Tobias went up to him with the fish-gall in his hand and blew it into his father's eyes, and took him by the arm and said: "It will be all right, father". Then when he had put the medicine on and applied it, using both hands he peeled off the patches from the corners of Tobit's eyes. Tobit flung his arms round him and burst into tears. "I can see you, my son, the light of my eyes!"' (Tob 11.11–14). In the meantime, Sarah arrives. 'It was a day of joy for all the Jews in Nineveh . . .' (Tob 11.17).

After the marriage-feast Tobias wants to give his fellow traveller half of everything he had brought with them. The angel says: ' "When you and Sarah prayed, it was I who brought your prayers into the glorious presence of the Lord . . . I am Raphael, one of the seven angels who stand in attendance on the Lord and enter his glorious presence . . ." . . . and when they rose to their feet he was no longer to be seen. They sang hymns of praise to God, giving him thanks for these great deeds he had done when his angel appeared to them' (Tob 12.12–21). That is the ending of the marvellous tale of the 'accompanying angel'.

I do not know that it is not an account of an historical event. Most probably it is not. Does that mean that it is a legend? I think it must be. A legend is an interpretation of life. It has its own truth, but it can be just as 'true' as history. A legend is always connected with an explanation of the meaning of life. Fairy tales, for example, can be more true than an historical account of something. They emphasize a few basic characteristics, and sometimes exaggerate them, but are more concerned to stress the really essential thing. We have to ask: What does it mean when we say that angels accompany us and are our companions?

A 'companion' is of course a friend who stays by our side on the way – if he is a guide he shows us the way. Perhaps he does it without any conscious knowledge or acknowledgement on our part that he is doing so. This enormous self-effacement is something that we have to learn from the angels. An angel helps us. He helps us, as in the case of Tobias, so that we are not seized by a 'fish'. He helps us to overcome wicked demons; indeed, he does more: he helps us to 'get our money back', to make a happy marriage, to help our father and, finally, to live in joy. An angel confers solid benefits on us. He doesn't bring us an 'ideal' love, but gifts of our earth. An angel is our companion in the sense that he accompanies us as the men we are.

When we talk of a 'companion', we should remember that a companion enters into, 'comes down into', our everyday life. He ought to share in our cares and worries, in our needs; he should rejoice at our marriage, at our father's recovery, and even that our dog is wagging his tail. This becoming quite natural of the supernatural is one of the greatest and most impressive characteristics of angels. They know what human existence means. In spite of the shortcomings apparent to us, our human existence is very meaningful to God. That is why it is possible for angels to be at our service. Not angels but men are the apex of creation. That may seem strange at first thought, but remember that Jesus did not become an angel but a man.

Perhaps we should think ourselves more deeply into the mystery. The angels are messengers in the unusual sense that they bring with them the person who sent them: God himself. Therefore we can say that God himself 'serves' us. That is the state of tension in which Jesus lives. He should serve God, and yet God serves him. It would

21

be presumptuous to try to exhaust so profound a mystery in so short a meditation. Insight is always the fruit of prayer.

Mighty angels

Mighty angels

As Romano Guardini once remarked in a book on the angels in Dante's *Divine Comedy*, the way people feel now and the ruling ideas of the modern age have made the angels weak and sometimes even ambiguous beings. If anyone wants to see what they really are and where they stand in Christian life, he has to put out of his mind almost everything that the art of the last five to six centuries (to say nothing of the devotional kitsch industry) has made of angels.

Guardini proposes a reading of the Bible. Perhaps a Christian should start by returning to the Old Testament. For example, he should read deeply and meaningfully the story of Jacob's struggle with an angel (Gen 32. 22–31). Or the account of an angel standing before Joshua and ordering him to take off his sandals in God's holy place (Jos 5.13–15). Of course the angelic figures in the New Testament reach supreme heights, all the way to that mighty angel who comes down from heaven in the Book of Revelation: 'He was wrapped in cloud, with the rainbow round his head; his face shone like the sun and his legs were like pillars of fire . . . His right foot he planted on the sea, and his left on the land. Then he gave a great shout, like the roar of a lion . . . ' (Rev 10.1–3).

The
mighty
angel

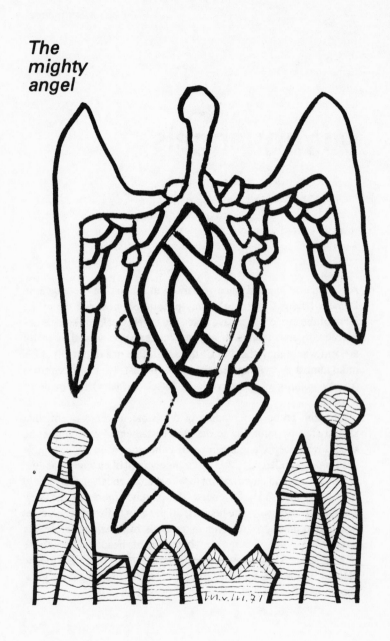

Mark tells us what can become of that kind of mighty being: 'So they came to the other side of the lake, into the country of Gerasenes. As he stepped ashore, a man possessed by an unclean spirit came up to him from among the tombs where he had his dwelling ... When he saw Jesus in the distance, he ran and flung himself down before him, shouting loudly, "What do you want with me, Jesus, son of the Most High God? ..." (For Jesus was already saying to him, "Out, unclean spirit, come out of this man!") Jesus asked him, "What is your name?" "My name is Legion", he said, "there are so many of us". ... Now there happened to be a large herd of pigs feeding on the hill-side, and the spirits begged him, "Send us among the pigs and let us go into them" ... and the unclean spirits came out and went into the pigs; and the herd, of about two thousand, rushed over the edge into the lake and were drowned ... the man who had been possessed begged to go with him. Jesus would not allow it, but said to him, "Go home to your own folk and tell them what the Lord in his mercy has done for you". The man went off and spread the news ... of all that Jesus had done for him; and they were all amazed' (Mk 5.1–20).

I have to admit that the whole series of events sounds rather strange. But what is related here by Mark is in fact necessary for an understanding of the Bible. Jesus sees an evil power behind the diseased body and soul. In fact there is an entire legion of demons there. A basic component of Jesus' messianic understanding of himself is the conviction that he has to contend with satanic forces. He knows very well that he is sent to break the powers who oppose the will of God. Satan is no primordial power, but a fallen creature who has entered into rebellion and tries to set up a kingdom of despair in opposition to God. But Jesus upholds salvation, unclouded and unmistakable. Behind the outwardly perceptible struggle against a visible opponent an invisible struggle is taking place.

We have to remember that Satan too is an angelic being. Even the men he holds in his clutches are of no small stature. In a pre-war book on Job, a now-forgotten writer called Peter Lippert said:

'With such men he brings about the most visible and conspicuous events on earth – what we call world-history ... The Enemy always appears wherever something great and wonderful is occurring in Your world, where the centuries are trammelled, or tempests and earthquakes are unleashed before which creation shudders ... Even Your Saviour, in whose form You appeared on earth, was confronted with the Devil ... And this demon was allowed the honour of addressing his ultimately decisive question to Your Anointed'.

Nature of angels

Nature of angels

In the Old Testament angels are fearsome, mighty beings. The New Testament rather tones down the might and power. Nevertheless the impression an angel gives is still one of superhuman bigness. The first thing he says to men is always 'Don't be afraid'.

Angels are mighty and therefore frightening. But they don't want to destroy men. The angels are in an unattainable location above mankind. For men they signify a boundary; a dividing-line at which it is possible to sense what earthly life is not. They are withdrawn from us. For the poet Rainer Maria Rilke, the angels are 'terrifying', 'almost deadly'. Man is no match for this terrible angelic nature. The stature of an angel is something to be measured in cosmic terms. Yet these majestic beings also relate to human history. The angels have to do with that aspect of our world which is governed by cause and context. And here, I am afraid, I must go just a short way into the realm of supposition.

It is only in our idea-world that the angels have become insipid. In the biblical context, they do not come to us 'privately', on their own account. Instead God himself is active and effective in them. For example, three men enter Abraham's tent; they are (or at least one of them is) 'the Lord' (Gen 18.1–33). Man cannot bear to see an angel's countenance. The angels are beings whose power extends beyond that of men. By nature they are orientated towards world history, whose ministers they are. They acknowledge neither boundaries of space nor barriers of time. Angels 'fly'. If we use 'world' in the sense of 'universe', or everything, then angels also belong to this creation. We call the angels 'spirits'. As Romano Guardini remarks, as a spirit an angel belongs to creation; the angels comprise its uppermost level. Yet angels do not yet belong to the Kingdom of God, even though they are in the presence of God.

One thing is very clear: Jesus introduced a new era in world history. The old order was replaced by a new one. Jesus' arrival was the coming of a new order, in which Jesus superseded intermediary powers. They lost their faculty of government for ever. The main text which supports this interpretation is in Paul: 'On that cross he discarded the cosmic powers and authorities like a garment; he made a public spectacle of them and led them as captives in his triumphal procession' (Col 2.15). Those powers Jesus threw off were the spirits to whom man had been subject: 'During our minority we were slaves to the elemental spirits of the universe ... Formerly when you did not acknowledge God, you were the slaves of beings which in their nature are no gods. But now that you do acknowledge God – or rather, now that he has acknowledged you – how can you turn back to the mean and beggarly spirits of the elements? Why do you propose to enter their service all over again?' (Gal 4.3–9). Christ cancelled the old world order. Jesus himself is our only angel. God set Jesus 'far above all government and authority, all power and dominion, and any title of sovereignty that can be named, not only in this age but in the age to come. He put everything in subjection beneath his feet ... ' (Eph 1.21–22). What these texts are really talking about is the dethronement of the angels – the good angels as well as the bad ones.

Angels of
revelation

Angels of revelation

The angels of revelation are not pretty, small or dainty creatures. They are so far above everything human that when they enter our realm of existence they tend to threaten us by the very majesty of their being. They are the light and ardour of creation, and the essence of all feeling and emotion. They are worshippers of the most profoundly concentrated power. They are searchers of the depths of divinity. They straddle, plumb and span the whole realm of earth. In the area of human existence an angel is universally pervasive and penetrative; we conceive of this power as an angel's ability to fly.

The angels are in God's presence. But that means that they are present everywhere. In Pauline theology they are 'principles of the world' from which things so to speak project, in order to show us how they really look. There are angels behind things, circumstances and historical events. They are present to us everywhere and incessantly, in the full immediacy of being. Hence our world is holy and the inner space of creation is already paradise. Occasionally in selected places, the angels' presence becomes denser, and makes them directly apprehensible. That is obvious for instance in children and the weak and defenceless. Behind the

Duet of
heaven and earth

defenceless, but above all behind children, who are also given to us in a defenceless state (Jesus has told us this), stands God himself in the form of an angel. If we do anything to harm them, we touch upon something that leads directly to the hidden mystery of God. Hence the unmistakable and sacred dignity of all those who are unable to defend themselves.

Because it is a defenceless creature, a child is a density point for the presence of angels in this world. The same is true of all that is undefended. An angel is especially present where defencelessness happens as it were from the innermost core of creation, where being is tender and holy, and where life is directed inwards. There heaven opens up to us. This is an appropriate point to summarize all that has so far emerged about angels. An angel always brings help; he is a saviour in need; he always has a special task for us. He wants to be our friend and to show us the way. He is in the presence of God and from that centre of divine tenderness he helps all those who are defenceless, and children especially. But Jesus has dethroned all the angels, good or bad. He himself has become our angel, our only mediator with God. Jesus himself has opened up heaven for us.

Hierarchy of angels

Hierarchy of angels

Although it seems contrary to what I have already said to talk of a hierarchy, or of choirs and categories of angels, I do so for good reasons: the greatest of the ancient Fathers of the Church and the foremost medieval theologians did so repeatedly and emphatically. And there are indications (at the very least) of such a notion in the Bible. There is a profound truth in the idea. Thomas Aquinas, for instance, says in his *Summa contra gentes*: 'The highest and first angelic beings see the basis of the order or providence as lying in its ultimate goal, which is the goodness of God. But some see more clearly than others. Those who see more clearly are called *Seraphim*, the ardent and burning ones, because to be designated in terms of fire associates one with the depth of love or of longing, and love and longing are directed towards the ultimate goal. Therefore Dionysus the Areopagite says that this name indicates both their ardent immutability in regard to the Divine and their versatility in guiding those below them to God as the ultimate goal. Those in the second rank fully acknowledge the ground of providence in the essential form of the Divine itself. They are called *Cherubim*, which may be interpreted as "fulness of knowledge", in other words, knowledge is fulfilled through the essential form of the knowable. Therefore Dionysus says that this designation means that they are observers of the primal creative power of divine beauty. Those of the third rank contemplate the enactment of divine justice. They are called *Thrones*, for the power of judgment is shown by the throne. Hence Dionysus says that this designation means that they are bearers of God and wholly capable of undertaking all that is divine.

'Among the lower spirits who receive from the higher spiritual beings a full knowledge of the divine order that they are to accomplish, there must be a hierarchy. For providence is enacted through many agents; through the order of *Dominions*. It is the concern of those who exercise dominion to command what others should do. Hence Dionysus says that the name ''Dominion'' indicates leadership in one's own right, removed from all serfdom and subjection'.

'Second, the enactment of providence . . . is extended through many agencies; and through the order of *Powers*. This order, as Dionysus says, indicates courage and maturity in all godly action, that no godly movement may languish in inertia. Clearly the primal ground of comprehensive action relates to this order of angels. Therefore it would seem that this order is entrusted with the movement of the heavenly bodies. From them as from inclusive causes there derive the particular operations of nature; hence they are also known as ''heavenly powers'', meaning that the celestial powers will be shaken (Lk 21.26). These spirits would also seem to be entrusted with those godly works which occur outside the order of nature, for which reason this is the highest of the divine services. Gregory says: ''Those spirits are called Powers through whom signs are mostly given''. And if there is anything else that is inclusive and primary among the divine tasks which are to be carried out, then it falls by rights to the lot of this order of angels.

'Third, the general order of providence, once it has taken effect, is unerringly preserved, and whatever could disturb that order is prevented. That is the concern of the order of *Powers*. Hence Dionysus says that the name ''Powers'' means well-ordered and precise enactment of what has been received from God. And

Gregory says that this order is entrusted with the task of keeping adverse forces in check.

'The lowest among the higher spirits are those who receive the order of divine providence from God, so far as it is recognizable in its particular causes. These spirits are placed directly over human affairs. Among human affairs are to be understood all lower beings and especially causes which are ordered in regard to man and serve the purposes of men. And among these spirits too there is a hierarchy. In other words, in human affairs there is a general good which is the welfare of the state or nation. That would seem to be the concern of the order of *Princes*. Hence Dionysus says that the name "Prince" indicates rule together with holy order. The Book of Daniel names Michael as the Prince of the Jews together with the (angel) Prince of the Persians and the Prince of the Greeks (Dan 10.20). Hence the order of kingdoms and the transition from one tribe to another must be part of the work of this order of angels. It would also seem to be the office of this order to instruct those who are among men about all that concerns the exercise of rule'.

'There is also a human good which is not located in the community but concerns the individual man in himself, but which is nevertheless of use not merely to one but to many men, as for instance that which is to be believed and followed by all as well as the individual; i.e., the worship of God, or similar things. That is the concern of *Archangels* who, Gregory says, announce the highest things. Hence we call Gabriel the Archangel because he announced the incarnation of the only-begotten Word, in whom all men must believe. But other matters have more to do with the individual. They are the concern of the order of *Angels*. Gregory says that they have to impart lesser things. They are also known as the guardians of men, in accordance with Scripture: "For he has charged his angels to guard you wherever you go" (Ps. 91.11)'.

I have quoted this somewhat dry text from Aquinas in full in order to show any unprejudiced reader that nowadays 'angelic theory' or "angelology" can't be taken to such extreme lengths and yet that this text, read attentively, has much to say about man as he really is.

Much could be said about the sometimes quasi-magical notion of 'providence', which serves as a principle of order for the entire hierarchical system (I have done so elsewhere, and refer the reader to my book *Prayer* for a more profound analysis of the concept).

I want to say something more about those mysterious beings in whom truth has become a living thing; about the angelic beings who live holy truth – the *Cherubim*. Above all, because truthfulness has suffered much in our times. What exactly are those beings whose life consists not only in uttering but in being truth? We must remember that truth is sorely threatened because of its inward gentleness. The higher the degree of truth, the 'weaker' its direct, compulsive strength and the more the spirit must open up to it in freedom. The nobler truth is, the more easily it can be shoved to one side, or laughed away in the face of harsh reality. That applies to all truth, but in a special degree to the sacred variety. In this sense, cherubim do not and should not announce individual truths. Their stature for us should be above all truths, should be *the* truth. These angels are not so to speak members of the company of philosophers, promoting an improved philosophy; or moralists who proclaim a more refined ethics; or any such thing. They want to open our eyes so that we can see. They want to establish a special point in us, from which we can take our bearings and from which we can project back upon God human existence and all its truths. The cherubim wish to give us the strength needed for that task.

You need courage nowadays to talk about that kind of truth: about a truth which illuminates all truths. The words used for talking about it, the trains of thought customary for the subject, are often devalued and debased of meaning. The boundaries of earthly existence, its disguises and pressures, would have to disappear in order if we wished to stand solely in *the* truth. For that, not just now and then, but by the very nature of the case, something is needed beyond the abovementioned tenderness and gentleness – something I have to call *severity*.

How intimately related things are when you look at them as a Christian; how simple they are in essence. Gentleness and severity, mildness and justice, goodness and discipline, gaiety and moderation. All those things come together in one thing, and the proper name for that one thing is love. If all those things are seen in the light of the New Testament revelation, and particularly in the sense of Jesus' statement, 'I am the truth' (Jn 14.6), then we see Jesus Christ the Cherubim: that is, the cherubim as a sign, standing for Christ himself. The same is true of the Old Testament.

The doctrine concerning the various choirs and hierarchies of angels is fulfilled in Christ; they are the various functions of Christ himself.

Guardian angels

Guardian angels

St Bernard, in a commentary on the passage from Psalm 91 about the angels, points out an important function of the angels: They protect us. ' "He has charged his angels . . ." ' An extraordinary condescension and truly a great proof of love. Who has charged? Whom? Why? What? Let us consider this great event carefully, brothers. Let us imprint it in our minds . . . The angels obey God. He has charged his angels to guard you wherever you go. They do not hesitate to carry you on their hands. The Lord has ordered the angels, his angels. For your sake, he has commanded those exalted and glorious beings, those who are close to him and joined to him in truth. But who are you . . . ? What has he commanded for your sake. That they guard you'.

That is a simple text, wholly in accordance with the spirit of the Bible. I know that theologians give every individual human being (but especially children) a 'guardian angel'. Some theologians even go so far as to allow several of them to each of us. Even Jesus spoke about children in this connexion.

But I want to look at the question from another viewpoint: that of our existential situation.

Man as such requires a higher power to protect him. Man is

49

essentially *homeless*. He looks everywhere for profundity and does not find it. Sometimes meetings – encounters – make us richer, and fill us with happiness and joy. But for the most part they empty us, make us wearier, and in a true and deep sense 'less'; they diminish us.

Take for example that noble arousal of the heart that we call *love*. It belongs among the true high points of our existence. I am far from contesting its great dignity. God made man to love. But anyone who has experienced genuine love knows how difficult it is to persist in it. Ultimately a condition can develop in which being together does not mean that love has given people unity and security, but that it has just put two solitaries together. It often happens that a love which consisted of a man or woman feeling really at home with another, doesn't come off. In this sense, some writers say, the true lover is not he or she who finds fulfilment, but he or she who remains unfulfilled and yet maintains love unflinchingly. Much more could be said about the tragic nature of love, but I want only to suggest the deep truth that genuine, fulfilling and wholly fulfilled love, a love which lasts, can be protected, encouraged and – despite all difficulties – brought to completion by something higher.

And what about the things of this world? – by which I mean all the events and moments of destiny in our lives? I must emphasize again how beautiful the things of the world can be; how fulfilling a task, how enthralling a properly completed piece of work, and how full of promise our destiny can sometimes be. Ever and again something externally real wishes to enter man's heart. All these 'things' are a task for him. But unfortunately, more often than not, man doesn't even hear this commission. Often, very often, he can't prolong the fulfilling moment. He is always expecting, always as it were absent-minded, hoping for something greater and even more fulfilling. He doesn't feel what is happening to him now as what it really is in itself, but as if it announced the fulfilment of a desire. Hence he thinks not of the 'things' but of himself. Something annihilating and negating holds sway within him. Where can he find room for 'things'? Essentially he can't give them house room. Even in the innermost depths of his very being homelessness rules him. For man is homeless not only in the external world; even in his very inwardness he is a refugee. A higher power must stand by him, if in the quick-flowing stream of things, only for a few seconds, he is to stop and look with open eyes at the beauty of the world and the immensity of the task before him, and if he is wholly to absorb them.

All that happens not only in our slight lives but in the existence of the saints. They were directly orientated to God. They often directly heard his call and gave themselves up to him. Does that mean that they found human fulfilment? Much could be said on the subject. I would refer the reader to some fragments from the *Pensées* of Pascal, which adequately express the tragic nature of that kind of attachment to God. Fragment 843 begins with the words: 'This is not the country of truth. It wanders unrecognized among men. God has wrapped it in a veil'. According to fragment 194, Christianity teaches that men live in darkness and at a distance from God; that that accords with the name he gives himself in Scripture:

Deus absconditus – the hidden or absent God. But for the same reason man is hidden from himself: 'He is so little aware of the nature of God that he does not know what he is himself' (fragment 430). Pascal is even harsher in fragment 548: 'We do not know what our life is, or our death, or what God or we ourselves may be'. Our God has, it seems, 'left' us: 'We ourselves cannot judge what is possible and impossible for God in relation to us. In truth, not only *Deus*, but *homo absconditus*, and man is hidden because God is'. A very pessimistic side of Pascal's apprehension of God is apparent here. I am very far from sharing this feeling of Pascal's. Nevertheless I admit that there is at least a core of truth in the fragments I have quoted. If that is so, how can a saint spend his life with a God who is 'hidden' to that extent, yet makes a direct claim on him? We know from the lives of many saints that they often felt abandoned by their God, and had to live through a 'dark night' – a dark night of the soul. But I think that was an essential part of their sanctity. Surely a higher power protected them and always gave them the strength to keep going.

*'I guard you wherever
you go'.*

Finally there is homelessness before God. I should perhaps stress the fact that for me God is *the* fulfilling power, and that he can bring men to joy and bliss. But danger threatens. The danger of exasperation. Romano Guardini put it very clearly when he wrote: 'Exasperation is the expression of human irritation at God. Irritation at the most essential aspect of God – his sanctity. Exasperation is revolt against the living essence of God. In the depth of the human heart, next to longing for the eternal source, from which creation comes, and in which alone all completion is to be found, there lies dormant resistance to the same God; a resistance which is the basic form of sin awaiting its opportunity. Of course exasperation seldom appears naked, as open rebellion against God's holiness. It usually conceals itself by directing itself against a man who bears that holiness: against the prophets, the apostles, the saints, the devoutly pious. People like that annoy us intensely. Something in us just can't stand that kind of dedicated life. That something protests and justifies itself with the always available insufficiencies of mankind. Man's sinfulness, say: a sinner surely can't be a vehicle of holiness! Or his weaknesses, which turn to wickedness in the perspective of rejection. Or the peculiarities of the saint. In short, the fact that he is a man and finite'.

A lot could be said about the various dangers of encounter with God. They are the great mysteries of our life. To survive them men need a higher form of aid: assistance that we simply can't count on in the human realm.

Here, too, Jesus shows himself to be our guardian angel. Jesus brought everything to unity and gave us the grace to experience God's closeness in human form, to be holy, to live things in their original holiness, and to love with all the effort of all his life. He conquered everything that in us takes the form of homelessness. He stands in a direct relationship to every single man, helping him and accompanying him. In that way our Lord Jesus is our only guardian angel.

Bad angels

Bad angels

Of course the teaching about the devil, the 'fallen angel', sounds rather strange at first. The easiest solution – as professors and theologians have suggested – would be to demythologize the whole doctrine.

Admittedly there is a lot of mythology in the biblical reports about the devil, the story of the good angels' fight with him, the fall of the angels, and such cures as the driving of a devil from a man.

Much of that has been taken over from other religions. But at the same time we have to recognize this: Jesus acknowledges that he is sent against Satan. With God's love he is to burst the bonds of self-seeking and hatred. With God's truth he is to illumine the darkness cast by the devil. With God's constructive power he is to conquer the devastation brought about by evil. With his holy purity he is to clarify the sordidness which Satan effects in that feeling creature, man. We cannot remove this basic fact of Jesus' life if he is to be understood honestly. Certainly, in the history of faith and piety, there has been much that was odd and offbeat, even stupid and absurd. Getting rid of all that and opposing it honestly, is not only our Christian duty, but a genuine act of piety.

Three biblical texts show Jesus himself as the victor over Satan.

The first comes from Mark's gospel: 'The doctors of the law, too, who had come down from Jerusalem, said, "He is possessed by Beelzebub", and "He drives out devils by the prince of devils". So he called them to come forward, and spoke to them in parables: "How can Satan drive out Satan? If a kingdom is divided against itself, that kingdom cannot stand; if a household is divided against itself, that house will never stand; and if Satan is in rebellion against himself, he is divided and cannot stand; and that is the end of him"'. And now comes the decisive verse: 'On the other hand, no one can break into a strong man's house and make off with his goods unless he has first tied the strong man up; then he can ransack the house' (Mk 3. 22–27).

The second text runs parallel to the foregoing. It comes from Matthew:' . . . if it is by the Spirit of God that I drive out the devils, then be sure the kingdom of God has already come upon you. Or again how can anyone break into a strong man's house and make off with his goods, unless he has first tied the strong man up before ransacking the house?' (Mat 12.28–29).

My third text is very unusual and comes from Revelation: 'Then I saw an angel coming down from heaven with the key of the abyss and a great chain in his hands. He seized the dragon, that serpent of old, the devil or Satan, and chained him up for a thousand years; he threw him into the abyss, shutting and sealing it over him, so that he might seduce the nations no more till the thousand years were over. After that he must be let loose for a short while . . . When the thousand years are over, Satan will be let loose from his dungeon; and he will come out to seduce the nations in the four quarters of the earth and to muster them for battle, yes, the hosts of Gog and Magog, countless as the sands of the sea. So they marched over the breadth of the land and laid siege to the camp of God's people, and the city that he loves. But fire came down on them from heaven and consumed them; and the devil, their seducer, was flung into the lake of fire and sulphur, where the beast and the false prophet had been flung, there to be tormented day and night for ever'. (Rev 20, 1–3; 7–10). Certainly this third text is more difficult to understand than the other two. One has to be familiar with the apocalyptic mode of expression. I cannot go into that in more detail in this book, but I must remind the reader that Revelation is not to be read as a history book. Everything that is told in it as part of a series of events is to be understood existentially, as what happens continually in our lives.

This short piece will fit very well as an introduction to my thoughts about the bad angels. I should like to think about evil in the sense that Jesus 'enchained' and conquered it. In this sense too he appears as a mighty angel. The power of Christ is not only strong when opposed to the spirit of deception and the sordid but obviously superior to it. I should like now to develop these thoughts a little.

Fall of the angels

Fall of the angels

At this point I must raise the question of an extraordinary mystery – redemption. I know that 'the redemption' has various aspects and dimensions. But I want to examine only one of them: Jesus saved us by his failure. That seems a very odd thing to say, yet it fits the whole Gospel. Like every man, Jesus had a destiny and his destiny was primarily a failure. Now let us see what that has to do with the victory over Satan.

Jesus lived in a state of inward immovability. He maintained God's truth in full clarity. He never watered down the message he had to proclaim. Satan could never vanquish him, and therefore wished to destroy Jesus humanly. This was where he was very 'weak'. Humanly speaking, he couldn't 'win through'. But with a magnificence that only a God-man could manage, he brought about the inconceivable: he took the failure on himself and turned it into redemption. And so he could say: 'But courage! The victory is mine; I have conquered the world' (Jn 16.33). And again: 'Now is the hour of judgment for this world; now shall the Prince of this world be driven out' (Jn 12.31). Clearly the redemption was not to occur through a simple 'outburst' of divine power. The kenosis, the 'emptying' or severe 'making self nothing' of which Paul speaks

(Phil 2.7) means redemption, and victory over the bad angels. It means: Jesus would conduct the struggle weakly and inadequately and would not 'win' initially ('win' in the sense that darkness would be banished forthwith and the love in men's hearts would immediately shine forth). Or, more precisely, defeat had to become redemption.

In that way Jesus forced Satan to give up by allowing Satan to conquer him in his human aspects. Jesus saw evil as it was. The text from Matthew that I have already cited ends on a deadly serious note: 'He who is not with me is against me, and he who does not gather with me scatters. And so I tell you this: no sin, no slander, is beyond forgiveness for men, except slander spoken against the Spirit, and that will not be forgiven ... either in this age or in the age to come' (Mt 12.30–32).

I have often meditated hard on this text, not only because I find it a really terrible statement in itself, but because it just doesn't fit with the disposition of Jesus as we know it otherwise – with his attitude of forgiveness. But once I listened to my much revered teacher, Romano Guardini, preaching on this text. Instead of offering his interpretation from my own memory (which isn't so exact as it once was), I shall quote the corresponding passage from his book *The Lord*: 'What has happened here? These people have slandered the Holy Spirit. They have not only set themselves against God, against his commandment, against his rule; not only against Christ, his person, word and deeds – but against the Spirit of God. Against his heart. Against his attitude. Against his way of thinking ... against the way in which he acts in regard to himself and men ... Think of human affairs ... You can imagine a friend injuring a friend because he is careless, judging him unjustly, saying something harsh that happens to catch him on a sore spot, or something like that. Anything of that kind can endanger friendship, according to the extent of the unkindness or its importance. But it would be a quite different affair were the friend to attack not just the work, words or behaviour but the fundamental way of thinking of his friend; if he said to him, for instance: Your heart is deceitful; your mind is evil; your intentions are impure. If anyone made such

... through your humility ...

accusations in all seriousness, then the friendship would collapse
... Something of that kind is in question here. In Jesus the
innermost intention and attitude of God are at work. To say that
here Satan is actually at work is tantamount to speaking out of an
absolutely evil will. Only someone whose spirit is inwardly seized
by darkness and agrees with that condition could speak in that way.
Here forgiveness is impossible because something has entered in
that leads beyond the earthly condition of man – ultimate
confirmation in evil'.

Something similar can happen to us if we do not accept the
mystery of the saving action of Jesus – his way of thinking, his
attitude: redemption through defeat. But Jesus knows how to
protect us from that. We must experience inwardly the profundity
of Paul's words and meditate on them constantly: 'Let your bearing
towards one another arise out of your life in Christ Jesus. For the
divine nature was his from the first; yet he did not think to snatch at
equality with God, but made himself nothing, assuming the nature
of a slave. Bearing the human likeness, revealed in human shape,
he humbled himself, and in obedience accepted even death – death
on a cross. Therefore God raised him to the heights and bestowed
on him the name above all names, that at the name of Jesus every
name should bow – in heaven, on earth, and in the depths – and
every tongue confess, "Jesus Christ is Lord", to the glory of God
the Father' (Phil 2.6–11).

Temptation

Temptation

I have already mentioned Jesus' self-effacement. But it is also appropriate to talk of a similar effacement of the effects of Satan. I mean that there are processes of temptation in which the evil power uses dramatic methods. I shall say something about those later. Just now I want to discuss that quiet kind of temptation to which so many good men and women and good Christians are subject or which they don't even notice.

Let me take an example. A Christian lives piously and in devotion to God in his world. He practises his faith as 'religion'. That gives him pleasure. He doesn't want to be a pharisee and probably doesn't judge other people who don't behave in the same way as he does. Perhaps he is successful in life and ascribes this success in part to his piety. He is quite content with himself and with his God. But this very self-satisfaction is dangerous. If a man is self-satisfied, God himself can do nothing or very little. And in this way, little by little, the man edges towards a slippery slope. Perhaps he commits no apparent grave sin in the process.

In Luke Jesus talks about service in humility. 'Suppose one of you has a servant ploughing or minding sheep. When he comes back from the fields, will the master say, "Come along at once and

Through your
self-effacement . . .

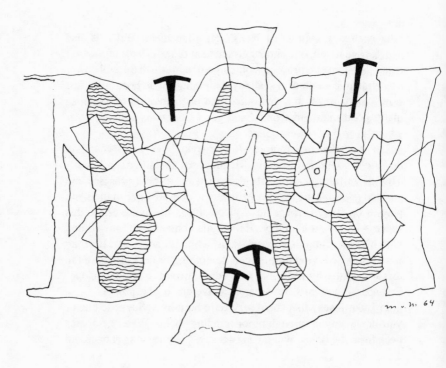

sit down"? Will he not rather say, "Prepare my supper, fasten your belt, and then wait on me while I have my meal; you can have yours afterwards"? Is he grateful to the servant for carrying out his orders? So with you: when you have carried out all your orders, you should say, "We are servants and deserve no credit; we have only done our duty"' (Lk 17.7–10).

At first we should forget the location of the example in the contemporary social environment. That is not important for us. Jesus had to speak like that if he wanted his audience to understand what he was saying. The core of this passage can be summarized as follows: Even when he has done everything that Jesus told him to do, a man must still be able to say: *I am an insignificant servant.* Not with any hypocrisy, not 'as if' he were one, but in all seriousness of life and conscience.

In addition we must remember that Jesus' commandments are not 'commandments' in the traditional sense of the term. For example, the Sermon on the Mount, the special ethics of Jesus, has certainly never been fully put into practice by anyone. His commandments are much more 'things to aim at': that is, signposts to a Christian way of life. As though Jesus said to us: I'm asking you to behave like this. I know that you'll never fulfil everything that I've asked for. But, when you come right down to it, that isn't what I'm after. I only want one thing: that you try to enter and live in that dimension which I have opened up for you. You'll fail in that every day, perhaps every hour. But if you continually pull yourself together and try at least to keep in the right direction, then you have already managed a great deal. Much more than most Christians. Even if you had done everything, you should say to yourself: *I'm an insignificant servant.*

From the foregoing it seems to me clear that Satan's real work of temptation occurs in the realm of quite sublime events. He wants to make men self-satisfied and in that way to wipe out Christ's spirit in them. That leads eventually to a form of existence that looks pious to outsiders, but is inwardly hard, stony, and no longer sensible to the movements of Jesus' heart. That is only *one* example. I leave it to the reader's imagination to find others,

Angels and men

perhaps from his own life. But I must ask him not to take them from others' lives. If he did that, he would already have succumbed to one of those 'seductive temptations' of the spirit of evil, and would be acting against the Spirit of Christ, who continually and emphatically commands us: Do not judge others!

Horror of evil

Horror of evil

From among the many biblical texts which describe the terrible power of evil, I shall choose only one, because it says a lot theologically (though in symbolic language). I shall give a short interpretation. It is the twelfth chapter of the Book of Revelation:

'Next appeared a great portent in heaven, a woman robed with the sun, beneath her feet the moon, and on her head a crown of twelve stars. She was pregnant, and in the anguish of her labour she cried out to be delivered. Then a second portent appeared in heaven: a great red dragon with seven heads and ten horns; on his heads were seven diadems, and with his tail he swept down a third of the stars in the sky and flung them to the earth. The dragon stood in front of the woman who was about to give birth, so that when her child was born he might devour it. She gave birth to a male child, who is destined to rule all nations with an iron rod. But her child was snatched up to God and his throne; and the woman herself fled into the wilds, where she had a place prepared for her by God, there to be sustained for twelve hundred and sixty days' (Rev 12.1–6).

Here is a universally effective representation of the birth of Jesus. The dragon is Satan. The imagery can be interpreted in various ways. At any rate the fearsome aspect of Satan, the desire of his power to annihilate everything, appears here in the middle of a depiction of the incarnation of God. Satan's awfulness is directed from the start against Jesus himself. Again I must stress the fact that Revelation is not a story or history in our sense. Everything there might well have happened – according to the opinion of some Fathers of the Church – right at the beginning of time, as though God had tested the angels by showing them the unique incarnation of the Son of God. But Lucifer refused, for he did not wish to serve the human being in Christ, a creature below him in the hierarchy of creation. From the start, therefore, the angelic revolt is to be seen in a Christological perspective.

'Then war broke out in heaven. Michael and his angels waged war upon the dragon. The dragon and his angels fought, but they had not the strength to win, and no foothold was left them in heaven. So the great dragon was thrown down, that serpent of old that led the whole world astray, whose name is Satan, or the devil – thrown down to the earth, and his angels with him. Then I heard a voice in heaven proclaiming aloud: ''This is the hour of victory for our God, the hour of his sovereignty and power, when his Christ comes to his rightful rule''. For the accuser of our brothers is overthrown, who day and night accused them before our God. By the sacrifice of the Lamb they have conquered him, and by the testimony which they uttered; for they did not hold their lives too dear to lay them down. Rejoice then you heavens and you that dwell in them! But woe to you, earth and sea, for the devil has come down to you in great fury, knowing that his time is short!' (Rev 12.7–12).

This is a symbolic description of the great 'fall of Satan'. First there is a battle with the dragon. Michael and his angels struggle against him and his followers (who are expressly called 'angels') and throw him down upon the earth. There is an unusual inconsistency in this text. On the one hand it says that there is no longer any room for them in heaven, and on the other hand that day and night Satan accused his brothers before God. I shall try to resolve this apparent contradiction in my next chapter. But at this point I should like to draw the reader's attention to the problem that

Satan was so to speak banned from heaven yet stood before God accusing the faithful. Then comes the last section:

'When the dragon found that he had been thrown down to the earth, he went in pursuit of the woman who had given birth to the male child. But the woman was given two great eagle's wings, to fly to the place in the wilds where for three years and a half she was to be sustained, out of reach of the serpent. From his mouth the serpent spewed a flood of water after the woman to sweep her away with its spate. But the earth came to her rescue and opened its mouth and swallowed the river which the dragon spewed from his mouth. At this the dragon grew furious with the woman, and went off to wage war on the rest of her offspring, that is, on those who keep God's commandments and maintain their testimony to Jesus' (Rev 12.13–7).

In this perspective and in the background the events on earth are dominated by a cosmic process. It is a question of whether men will let themselves be led astray. As far as heaven is concerned the story is already decided. Heaven has won. Now it is up to us men to show whether we opt for the commandments of God and the testimony of Jesus. The earth itself has already made its contribution in warding off a first attempt of Satan's. But now war is being waged against mankind. And this war will be no less frightful than its predecessor. But we saw that the real struggle is waged against Christ, against the God-Man, who united heaven and earth, the divine and the human, in himself. Hence we can say that since Christ as God has already conquered, the humanity that is essentially united with him will win through as well. Jesus is our saviour in all need, even the most terrible need.

Now I should like to undertake something that will perhaps cause some headshaking among readers. I want to defend the Devil.

Attempt at a defence

Attempt at a defence

First some biblical references: In the Book of Genesis Satan appears as the Tempter – portrayed as a serpent – in paradise (cf. Gen 3.1ff). In the Book of Job we read: 'The day came when the members of the court of heaven took their places in the presence of the Lord, and Satan was there among them. The Lord asked him where he had been. "Ranging over the earth", he said, "from end to end". Then the Lord asked Satan, "Have you considered my servant Job? You will find no one like him on earth, a man of blameless and upright life, who fears God and sets his face against wrongdoing". Satan answered the Lord, "Has not Job good reason to be God-fearing? Have you not hedged him round on every side with your protection, him and his family and all his possessions? Whatever he does you have blessed, and his herds have increased beyond measure. But stretch out your hand and touch all that he had, and then he will curse you to your face". Then the Lord said to Satan, "So be it. All that he has is in your hands; only Job himself you must not touch". And Satan left the Lord's presence'. (Job 1.6–12. It is put even more strongly in Job 2.1–7 – since there the Lord himself gives Job into the hands of Satan).

In the prophet Zechariah we read: 'Then he showed me Joshua

*If you can,
anchor your enemy
in love!*

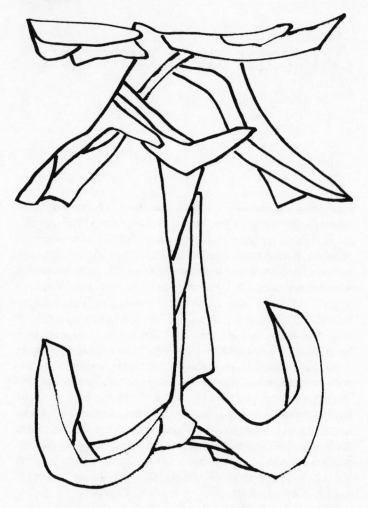

the high priest standing before the angel of the Lord, with the Adversary standing at his right hand to accuse him. The [angel of the] Lord said to the Adversary: "The Lord rebuke you, Satan, the Lord rebuke you who are venting your spite on Jerusalem"' (Zech 3.1–2).

In the Letter of Jude we read: '. . . when the archangel Michael was in debate with the devil . . . he did not presume to condemn him in insulting words, but said, "May the Lord rebuke you!"' (Jude 9).

Peter uses the same text in a somewhat altered though related context: 'They flout authority; reckless and headstrong, they are not afraid to insult celestial beings, whereas angels, for all their superior strength and might, employ no insults in seeking judgment against them before the Lord' (2 Pet 2.11).

Those are only a few biblical texts which state that the Devil and the fallen angels live in the same 'place' as the angels and the saints, have dealings with one another and have the right to speak to God himself. As I have already said elsewhere: it must be so. The fallen angels must experience God with their entire being. The fact that nevertheless they reject God is the very essence of their self-damnation. But one might ask: Do they all live in heaven? My answer must be Yes.

But this heaven is experienced from the basis of an inner disposition. One who has surrendered himself to God lives in total bliss. One who has set himself against God, finds heaven intolerable, experiences it as hell. Paul Claudel said once that hell is the inner imbalance of a spirit in its very depths.

Of course hell cannot exist as a 'place'. What God creates is undeniably good, for he can make something exist only in accordance with his nature. If it were not modelled on him it would be nothing. Hell consists essentially of the inner disposition of the heart. Just think of a fine Sunday. We wake up quite refreshed and go out for a walk. The weather is fine, the sun bathes the world in generous rays, the birds sing, and we are quite happy. Harmony and inward joy reign everywhere. But if we take a fish from the stream so that he too can enjoy this bliss, it turns to hell for him. He

Self-sacrifice

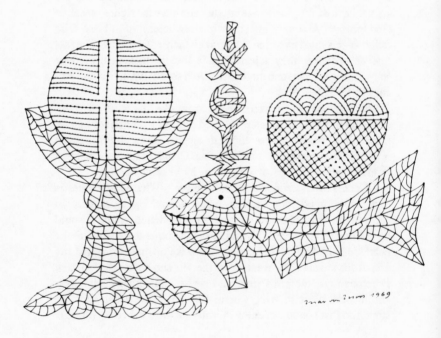

simply isn't used to this world; his whole constitution is different. I think in the same way of that process to which we have given the name 'hell'.

Let me pose a delicate question that I can't and won't try to answer: Is there a certain degree of happiness even in hell? Some years ago a theological journal carried an article on hell by a Dominican; it seemed very sensible to me at the time. At the end of the article he announced a sequel in which he promised to explain what this 'certain degree of happiness' might consist in. That could have meant a renewal of our whole theology and preaching about hell. But that second part never appeared. Someone stopped it – prevented the review from publishing it, that is. The reader should and can speculate about the possibility himself. That there must be a certain degree of joy and even a certain happiness in hell is quite clear. It is a constant teaching of the Church that neither an absolute nothing nor an absolute evil can exist. That statement (as far as I am concerned) resolves the basic question of whether joy and happiness can, indeed must, exist in hell. But what exactly that joy and happiness consist in is something I should not like to debate.

Another marginal thought – but this time even more tentative: God is infinite. Therefore he possesses an infinite number of mysteries. But he has revealed to us just enough of these mysteries to allow us with our weak powers to reach heaven. We must understand that properly: no less, but no more. He has reserved an infinitely great number of mysteries to himself. John says even of the actions of Jesus: 'There is much else that Jesus did. If it were all to be recorded in detail, I suppose the whole world could not hold the books that would be written' (Jn 21.25). God's method of acting in history was described by Gregory of Nyssa with the Greek word *akolouthia*. For Gregory *akolouthia* means the progressive development of the divine plan and of divine revelation in all its stages. He writes: 'Just as the first age of man, his infancy, is still fed with milk from the breast, which is followed by another nourishment that is appropriate for the infant until it matures, so, I believe, the soul partakes of natural life in an appropriate manner in each and every instance and according to a progressive order (*taxei*

85

kai akolouthia), while it partakes of the good things reserved for it in [eternal] bliss according to its power of comprehension' (PG 46.180A). Irenaeus of Lyons even saw that progress as applying to our life in heaven. These thoughts bring me, indeed compel me to ask, whether among the mysteries which God reserves for our comprehension there is not a solution to the problem of the 'bad angels'. Of course I'm not saying that that they *are* redeemed. I'm just asking the question. Perhaps God, whose self-abasement we have experienced in his incarnation, could carry out another self-effacement (of a kind inconceivable to us humans) which would allow those angels finally to find their way back to him. Perhaps there is some slight indication of that in Christ's words from the cross – in Mark the only words that he spoke from the cross: 'My God, my God, why hast thou forsaken me?' (Mk 15.34). I realize that that statement allows of several interpretations. Therefore I say that it is possible.

God is deeply moved by the tears of the fallen archangel. But he can do nothing (at least provisionally) against the angel's pride. Yet in the texts already quoted we constantly find that the angels, even the archangel Michael, did not presume to condemn in insulting words. Lucifer means bearer or bringer of light. And I hope with all my heart that the light that of his nature he bears within him will enlighten him. With that wish I shall close this chapter on the 'bad angels'. Of course there is still much I could say about them. Let us return instead to the good angels, because they have much more that is of value for our Christian life, and indeed for our human existence. But remember: We have seen that Jesus finally and for ever conquered and enchained Satan. It is in that perspective that we should consider evil – not in fear and anxiety, but with confidence and even thankfulness.

Eucharistic angels

Eucharistic angels

In the Roman eucharistic liturgy there is a very interesting prayer after the words of consecration. It is known as the *epiclesis*. Most of the eastern churches look on it as the actual consecration. We should at least see it as completing what was begun in the consecration. The prayer reads: 'Almighty God, we pray that *your angel* may take this sacrifice to your altar in heaven. Then, as we receive from this altar the sacred body and blood of your Son, let us be filled with every grace and blessing. Through Christ our Lord. Amen'. That is the fulfilment of the eucharist in which our whole faith is comprised and which is therefore also known as the *mysterium fidei*, the mystery of faith. Now the earthly and the heavenly altars coincide. The earth has become heaven.

Only Jesus Christ himself can do that. Therefore the great majority of liturgical scholars assume that the expression 'your angel' stands for Christ himself. I find that theologically perceptive and acceptable. Accordingly we can derive the attitude of the angels from the inner disposition which led Christ to institute the eucharist for us. I don't want in this context to enter into a discussion of the eucharist or communion or Jesus' sacrifice in a sacramental form, but simply to ask what could have been the inner attitude of our redeemer when at the threshold of death he presented us with his body and blood: that is, his entire living existence.

Jesus wanted to give his friends something. He sensed (for perhaps he did not quite realize) that his last hour had come. He had found out something which is true of all gifts: he gave himself. He so to speak stepped out of himself. For that purpose he took the least pretentious things in the world, bread and wine, which he transformed into his own existence, which he filled with his life, and which he gave to his friends. In that way he 'overcame' his own life, his last hour of fear and anguish, and his inner need.

At this point I must go a little deeper into what Christ meant by the eucharist. For centuries a very important aspect of the eucharist was obscured by abstract concepts. Theologians found words for this 'intensive presence' of Christ: 'trans-substantiation', and even (recently) 'trans-finalization'. Surely, in a meditation at least, it is a good idea to forget these terms and to consider the event itself. And that event was: Through a premonition of death Jesus became wholly 'himself'. He was that already. But possibly not in that intensity. Now he became wholly 'presence'. The eucharist as a mode of life always means presence. Whoever ventures to give himself is already eucharist for others, and eats and drinks their life. But we must remember something very important when we compare our self-giving, our presence, with that of Jesus: Jesus could give himself wholly. We cannot do that. In such moments we would recall all that is awry, dark and evil in our own existence, everything like that that is always within us. In all his responsibility, a lover asks whether in giving himself he is not presenting the other with his own wrong tendencies, with his own essential weakness. Only *one* man could quite consciously give all of us his entire being, all his feelings, thoughts and sensibility. That man was Jesus.

Insofar as we try to emulate the purity of the presence of Christ, some part of the eucharist occurs in us too: the transformation of our own being into the presence of God. Then we would become – if to a certain extent only, at least most assuredly – 'eucharistic angels' for our fellow men. Certainly our Lord Jesus, our only

Victory in and through defeat

'eucharistic angel', will be with us, helping us to realize our intention.

Creation of angels

Creation of angels

The biblical accounts of the creation of the angels are unsatisfactory testimony. That event has to be deduced from the nature of angels. Of course if I were to go about the matter logically and not meditatively, I would put this chapter at the beginning of the book. But seen from the viewpoint of its own particular, contemplative logic, it is wholly appropriate at this point. In meditation one has always to begin with what is easier to grasp.

Together with a large number of Christian theologians and philosophers, I see the first moment, the moment of the creation of the angels out of nothing, as comprising three inseparable aspects. All three occur in the same moment and are only separable in spirit.

The first aspect was creation from God. That was the creation 'only' of spirit, and of pure spirit at that. That which is specific to angels was not as yet fashioned. Scripture has nothing to say about such an angel. In his *Confessions* Augustine says of such beings (should they exist at all) that they exist in 'an insubstantial and wandering state of spiritual formlessness': *Spiritalis informitatis vagabunda deliquia* (*Conf* 13.5,6); that is, within they are still to some degree chaotic. Then this spirit is faced with a decision. Or, better, it is faced, for 'then' does not convey the inseparability of the moment. I have already spoken about what that test might be (in the chapter on the terrible aspect of evil) and I said there that God placed before the spirits the incarnation of his own Son: the becoming man of Christ to which they had to subordinate themselves. In that there occurred the third aspect – the moment of decision. Yet that decision was absolute. They decided in the very first moment of their existence. For angels are pure spirits and therefore simple. Their whole being was already comprised in their first action. That was the moment of clarity of consciousness, of awful freedom, of full self-realization. An act from which only the angel proper emerged as angel, but also the devil, who is really God's enemy and not only a 'demon'.

In his *Summa Theologica* Aquinas says that 'It is characteristic of the angelic nature that it does not achieve completion gradually, but that by virtue of its essence it possesses that realization immediately' (I, 52.5). We find something much the same (though not so clearly expressed in his *Commentary on the Sentences of Peter Lombard*: 'The end of man's road is his death. The end of the angel's road is the decision of its volitional choice, by which it plumps for good or evil. Just as after their death men persist in good or in evil, so do the angels after their decision for or against. But man has a longer road to travel than the angel, for man was set at a greater distance from God and must go in search of knowledge. But the angel, through his divinely-shaped understanding, could attain directly to the divine without any seeking' (2; d7,1,2).

I should like to draw on a superb text from Aquinas's *Summa Theologica* to bring home the essential points of the subject a little more surely. It is a very human and true passage, which we would do well to consider very carefully: 'Certain men even in this state of being on the way are greater than certain angels, not actually but virtually, inasmuch as they have such great love that they can merit a higher degree of beatitude than that possessed by certain angels. In the same way we might say that the seed of a great tree is virtually greater than a small tree, though actually it is much smaller' (I, 117.2 ad 3).

At the same time, we should meditate deeply on the story of

Created beings
like us

Jacob's wrestling: 'So Jacob was left alone, and a man wrestled with him there till daybreak. When the man saw that he could not throw Jacob, he struck him in the hollow of his thigh, so that Jacob's hip was dislocated as they wrestled. The man said, "Let me go, for day is breaking", but Jacob replied, "I will not let you go unless you bless me". He said to Jacob, "What is your name?", and he answered, "Jacob". The man said, "Your name shall no longer be Jacob, but Israel, because you strove with God and with men, and prevailed". Jacob said, "Tell me, I pray, your name". He replied, "Why do you ask me my name?", but he gave him his blessing there' (Gen 32.25–30). Jacob is alone and wakes up in the night. He seizes a 'man', one who awakens fear and is mysterious. He is the 'angel of the Lord', and therefore a finite being, yet, as verse 30 indicates, in some way God himself. The angels are 'messengers' of God in the odd sense that in some way they bring the Sender himself. And it is with such a mighty being that Jacob struggles throughout the night. He is defeated in the end only through the 'man's' supernatural strength. Even then Jacob doesn't let go until the 'man' blesses him. This extraordinary event shows how powerful a man can be, even when faced with an angel.

Finally, there is Jesus' incarnation. He did not become an angel but a man. He found Mary's womb much more worthy than the illumined spiritual space of an angelic being. Angels are sent by the Lord to serve us, and indeed the Lord Jesus himself serves us in them. Of course we must not forget that we should sometimes serve them, for we do not know who among them may be the Lord himself. 'Three men' entered Abraham's tent. Abraham showed them hospitality and behold, one of them was the Lord (Gen 18).

Angels and the
visible world

Angels and the visible world

In Newman's *Apologia pro vita sua* there is a very beautiful passage which conveys something very important for our theme: 'I suppose it was to the Alexandrian school, and to the early Church, that I owe in particular what I definitely held about the angels. I viewed them, not only as the ministers employed by the Creator in the Jewish and Christian dispensations, as we find on the face of Scripture, but as carrying on, as Scripture also implies, the Economy of the Visible World. I considered them as the real causes of motion, light, and life, and of those elementary principles of the physical universe, which, when offered in their developments to our senses, suggest to us the notion of cause and effect, and of what are called the laws of nature. I have drawn out this doctrine in my Sermon for Michaelmas Day, written not later than 1834. I say of the angels: "Every breath of air and ray of light and heat, every beautiful prospect, is, as it were, the skirts of their garments, the waving of the robes of those whose faces see God". Again, I ask what would be the thoughts of a man who, "when examining a flower, or a herb, or a pebble, or a ray of light, which he treats as something so beneath him in the scale of existence, suddenly discovered that he was in the presence of some powerful being who was hidden behind the visible things he was inspecting, who, though concealing his wise hand, was giving them their beauty, grace, and perfection, as being God's instrument for the purpose, nay, whose robe and ornaments those objects were, which he was so eager to analyze?'''

Newman remarks that the Old and New Testament sources say nothing about this aspect of the subject. That is not quite correct. Throughout the Bible there are reports of 'angelic visitations', when an angel or several angels appear visibly, in a living form, and sometimes even so that they can be grasped. On my hypothesis (that is, that Jesus has 'replaced' all angels), Newman's point is not so extraordinary as he himself seems to find it. I should like to make three additional points to enforce what he says.

First let us look at the texts from the New Testament which refer to Jesus' victory over the angels:

'[Christ is enthroned] far above all government and authority, all power and dominion, and any title of sovereignty that can be named, not only in this age, but in the age to come' (Eph 1.21).

'[He is the one] in whom our release is secured and our sins forgiven. He is the image of the invisible God; his is the primacy over all created things. In him everything in heaven and on earth was created, not only things visible but also the invisible orders of thrones, sovereignties, authorities, and powers: the whole universe has been created through him and for him. And he exists before everything, and all things are held together in him' (Col 1.14–17).

'Then comes the end, when he delivers up the kingdom to God the Father, after abolishing every kind of domination, authority and power. For he is destined to reign until God has put all enemies under his feet; and the last enemy to be abolished is death' (1 Cor 15.24).

'For he has forgiven us all our sins; he has cancelled the bond which pledged us to the decrees of the law. It stood against us, but he has set it aside, nailing it to the cross. On that cross he discarded the cosmic powers and authorities like a garment; he made a public spectacle of them and led them as captives in his triumphal procession' (Col 2.14–15).

'[Baptism] brings salvation through the resurrection of Jesus Christ, who entered heaven after receiving the submission of angelic authorities and powers, and is now at the right hand of God' (1 Pet 3.21–22).

The next step from there would be the teaching of Paul on the 'body' of Christ:

'He [God] put everything in subjection beneath his feet, and appointed him as supreme head to the church, which is his body and as such holds within it the fulness of him who himself receives the entire fulness of God' (Eph 1.22–23).

'No, let us speak the truth in love; so shall we fully grow up into Christ. He is the head, and on him the whole body depends. Bonded and knit together by every constituent joint, the whole frame grows through the due activity of each part, and builds itself up in love' (Eph 4.15–16).

'He is . . . the head of the body, the church. He is its origin, the first to return from the dead, to be in all things alone supreme. For in him the complete being of God, by God's own choice, came to dwell. Through him God chose to reconcile the whole universe to himself, making peace through the shedding of his blood upon the cross – to reconcile all things, whether on earth or in heaven, through him alone' (Col 2.9–10).

Before I present the third, decisive stage of this thought process, I should like to summarize the first two steps. First it became clear that Christ replaced all the good angels and conquered all the bad angels. Second: This 'Kyrios' makes himself a body from humankind. In a mysterious way we can all grow in him into a living unity, which is called the Church. Here we are to understand the term 'Church' in a very broad sense. I have often expressed my view that the statement 'There is no salvation without the Church' is quite consoling, for by all criteria of logic it can be put the other way, so that it says 'Wherever there is salvation, there is the Church'. *Ubi ecclesia, ibi salus.* But where salvation is, only God knows. From its beginnings the Church has been aware of 'members of the church' who know nothing of Jesus, and possibly even nothing of God, but who live honestly in accordance with their conscience. That has been called 'baptism of desire' – but I prefer the term 'baptism of longing'.

I see the third, conclusive and most important stage of the pertinent thought process in the statement in the Creed about Jesus' 'descent into hell'. That is the redemptive act proper of our Lord. Until now, however, people have only hinted that with Christ's death and resurrection heaven was opened up for those 'souls' who had died before Christ's death. But the term 'hell' is very inappropriate. Jesus was much more precise when he said: 'Jonah was in the sea-monster's belly for three days and three nights, and in the same way the Son of Man will be three days and three nights in the bowels of the earth' (Mt 12.40). The 'bowels of the earth' refers to that core from which all forms accost us, and present their visible living presence to us. Hence Christ attained to the innermost mystery of appearances and phenomena on this earth and – since people then still thought in terms of a system in which the earth was the centrepoint of the universe – the innermost mystery of all phenomena of the entire universe.

I could easily support these insights with texts from the Fathers of the Church, primarily from Irenaeus of Lyons, Clement of Alexandria, Origen, Gregory of Nyssa, and others, right up to Bonaventure, the theologian of the high Middle Ages, for whom the visible world was *corpus angelicum*, the body of angels. From this perspective, the Christology of Pierre Teilhard de Chardin, for whom the ultimate fulfilment meant 'Christ, built from human beings and surrounded by a glorified world', seems to fit the best theological traditions, especially in his emphasis on the irradiation or increasing transparency of the world to Christ.

*Experience the ultimate
in the provisional*

Angels of the
right moment

Angels of the right moment

The Acts of the Apostles tell of an event with important implications for our subject: 'Then the angel of the Lord said to Philip, "Start out and go south to the road that leads down from Jerusalem to Gaza". (This is the desert road.) So he set out and was on his way when he caught sight of an Ethiopian. This man was a eunuch, a high official of the Kandake, or Queen, of Ethiopia, in charge of all her treasure. He had been to Jerusalem on a pilgrimage and was now on his way home, sitting in this carriage and reading aloud the prophet Isaiah. The Spirit said to Philip, "Go and join the carriage". When Philip ran up he heard him reading the prophet Isaiah and said, "Do you understand what you are reading?" He said, "How can I understand unless someone will give me the clue?" So he asked Philip to get in and sit beside him.

'The passage he was reading was this: "He was led like a sheep to be slaughtered; and like a lamb that is dumb before the shearer, he does not open his mouth. He has been humiliated and has no redress. Who will be able to speak of his posterity? For he is cut off from the world of living men".

'"Now", said the eunuch to Philip, "tell me, please, who is it that the prophet is speaking about here: himself or someone else?"

109

Then Philip began. Starting from this passage, he told him the good news of Jesus. As they were going along the road, they came to some water. "Look", said the eunuch, "here is water: what is there to prevent my being baptized?"; and he ordered the carriage to stop. They both went down into the water, Philip and the eunuch; and he baptized him. When they came up out of the water the Spirit snatched Philip away, and the eunuch saw no more of him, but went happily on his way' (Acts 8.26–39).

An angel of the Lord, a Spirit and the Spirit of the Lord (we know, if my hypothesis is right, that he is Christ himself) intervenes three times in a series of events. First he gives Philip an indeterminate task, then he describes the task more precisely, and finally he snatches him away. All this has to do with a saving process which the Bible again and again calls *kairos.*

A *kairos* is the good or favourable moment for the grace of God. It is a time that man cannot determine by himself. In Isaiah, the Lord says: 'In the hour of my favour I answered you, and I helped you on the day of deliverance' (Is 49.8). This revelation is echoed in the New Testament: 'Sharing in God's work, we urge this appeal upon you: you have received the grace of God; do not let it go for nothing. God's own words are: "In the day of my favour I gave heed to you; on the day of deliverance I came to your aid"' (2 Cor 6. 1–2). In the Letter to the Hebrews we read: 'See to it, brothers, that no one among you has the wicked, faithless heart of a deserter from the living God' (Heb 3.13). And there is Jesus' own accusation: The Pharisees and Sadducees came, and to test him they asked him to show them a sign from heaven. His answer was: 'In the evening you say, "It will be fine weather, for the sky is red"; and in the morning you say, "It will be stormy today; the sky is red and lowering". You know how to interpret the appearance of the sky; can you not interpret the signs of the times?' (Mt 16.1–3).

In the Book of the Preacher (Qohelet or Ecclesiastes) there is a very fine text on the 'favourable time': 'For everything its season, and for every activity under heaven its time: a time to be born and a time to die; a time to plant and a time to uproot; a time to kill and a time to heal; a time to pull down and a time to build up; a time to weep and a time to laugh; a time for mourning and a time for dancing; a time to scatter stones and a time to gather them; a time to embrace and a time to refrain from embracing; a time to seek and a time to lose; a time to keep and a time to throw away; a time to tear and a time to mend; a time for silence and a time for speech; a time to love and a time to hate; a time for war and a time for peace . . . [God has made] everything to suit its time' (Eccles 3.1–11).

We should apply this teaching of the Bible about the *kairos,* the favourable time, the right moment, to our own lives, each in his own way. It is part of each individual grace, or *charisma,* to do so appropriately. But I should like to go a step further and claim that there are favourable moments even in the life of faith. God has not revealed once and for all in the history of humankind everything that man must know. God has been patient with us. He has let the fruit of truth ripen slowly. In my opinion it is unnecessary, indeed impossible, for anyone in any one life to emulate all God's truths at once. A man is entitled to delay the decision in the case of certain truths of faith – which can be quite fundamental truths. That does not imply any loss of faith, but rather leaving oneself time to mature. There is no denial of the certain truth of God. But one says to oneself: The right moment hasn't come for me yet to make God's truth my own by contributing my whole existence. But the *kairos* for this truth will come. One will sense the favourable moment, the time of grace. Then a Christian is duty-bound by virtue of his faith to steep himself in that truth, and to persist in it.

For the theologians among my readers I should like to say something about which Pope John XXIII was most emphatic. Even in the Church there is a favourable moment, even for very important truths of revelation. The activity of theologians – like the activity of every Christian – cannot be deduced from abstract norms. There is also something that Karl Rahner has called the 'historically apt imperative'. Even the individual theologian has his individual grace of thought. He is not bound to research all God's truths or to represent them all with the same insistence. He should deepen his comprehension of those points in revelation which God has presented to him as his particular task. If he isn't so inclined to

111

Show us the
right
moment!

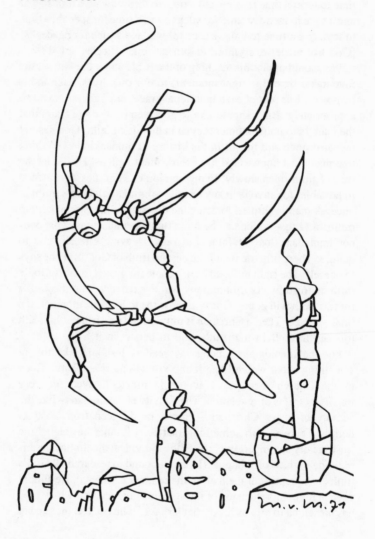

ponder other points (I am tempted to say, if he doesn't stray to other points), he will carry out God's work and represent the Church in his own individually grace-filled area.

The 'pastoral' teaching we can glean from the text cited is no less important than the 'theological' point. The pastor of souls should give time to those in his charge. He should show at least some part of God's patience with us. A great degree of compassion is called for from us in our Christian and ministerial attitude to others. But we are also required – and that is the meaning of an intelligent and practised cure of souls – to judge the right moment for the person in question. A Christian and especially a pastor should allow himself to be led by Jesus, by his 'angel', in seeking to discover what his relation to this or that man is at this or that moment of time. Then, however frail he may be, however unlettered in many things, even indeed if he is sinful, he will become an angel of God for this actual living man in his unique untransferable situation. The 'discovery' of the individual grace of God for a particular person is perhaps the most difficult but also the most urgent of pastoral tasks – yet how often we fail in that commission.

Angels of death

Angels of death

In his parable about the rich man and Lazarus, the poor man, Jesus says (so to speak as an aside): 'The poor man died and was carried away to be with Abraham' (Lk 16.22). It is easy to see behind the pious Jewish expression 'with Abraham' something like the 'heart of God'. In any case, angels carry poor Lazarus to a place of consolation.

The Acts of the Apostles tell of a strange smile on the face of the young martyr, the deacon Stephen: 'And all who were sitting in the Council fixed their eyes on him, and his face appeared to them like the face of an angel' (Acts 6.15, especially 7.56).

In the traditional Roman liturgical prayers for the dead, we read: 'Go forth, Christian soul, from this world in the name of God the almighty Father, who created you, in the name of Jesus Christ, the Son of the living God, who suffered for you, in the name of the Holy Spirit, who is poured out in you ... In the name of angels and archangels. In the name of thrones and dominions. In the name of princes and powers. In the name of cherubim and seraphim ... Towards your soul as it goes forth from the body, there hastens the glorious company of angels'.

According to these texts, in the very depths of human life, in death, there is an ultimate encounter with that which man has always sensed behind the things and events of the world and behind his own life. In essence, that is a meeting with Jesus Christ. From a theological viewpoint, in that moment man attains to his full capacity of decision. He is lovingly received, guided, led and borne up. Everything now depends on him alone. Christ does not reject him. If he expresses the Yes of his life, even if it seemed to be a 'wasted' life, he will be taken up into eternal bliss. Here I should like to protest against all representations in sermons and pictures of, or any idea of, an avenging angel. All revenge was decisively cancelled by Jesus Christ. Jesus always receives his creatures with love, wherever, whenever and however they come to him. To know that, to offer others that picture of death, is not only immensely liberating, but something that makes us like helping angels, like our Lord Jesus.

Angels of paradise

Angels of paradise

'I tell you, there is joy among the angels of God over one sinner who repents' (Lk 15.10). That is one of the most comforting statements in the New Testament. But first let us look back. Christ sends letters to the Christian communities. They are addressed to the 'angels' of the individual churches. Despite judgment, praise and threat, these letters always contain words of promise. In the letter to the angel of Ephesus, we read: 'To the angel of the church at Ephesus write: ... Hear, you who have ears to hear, what the Spirit says to the churches! To him who is victorious I will give the right to eat from the tree of life that stands in the Garden of God' (Rev 2.1–7). To the angel of Smyrna: 'Only be faithful till death, and I will give you the crown of life. Hear, you who have ears to hear, what the Spirit says to the churches! He who is victorious cannot be harmed by the second death' (Rev 2.10–11). To the angel of Pergamum: 'Hear, you who have ears to hear, what the Spirit says to the churches! To him who is victorious I will give some of the hidden manna; I will give him also a white stone, and on the stone will be written a new name, known to none but him who receives it' (Rev 2.17). To the angel of Thyatira: 'To him who is victorious, to him who perseveres in doing my will to the end, I will

give authority over the nations . . . and he shall rule them with an
iron rod . . . and I will give him also the star of dawn' (Rev
2.26–28). To the angel of Sardis: 'He who is victorious shall thus
be robed all in white; his name I will never strike off the roll of the
living, for in the presence of my Father and his angels I will
acknowledge him as mine' (Rev 3.5). To the angel of Philadelphia:
'He who is victorious – I will make him a pillar in the temple of my
God; he shall never leave it, and I will write the name of my God
upon him, and the name of the city of my God, that new Jerusalem
which is coming down out of heaven from my God, and my own
new name' (Rev 3.12). And the seventh letter is to the angel of
Laodicea: 'Here I stand knocking at the door; if anyone hears my
voice and opens the door, I will come in and sit down to supper with
him and he with me. To him who is victorious I will grant a place on
my throne, as I myself was victorious and sat down with my Father
on his throne. Hear, you who have ears to hear, what the Spirit says
to the churches!' (Rev 3.20–22).

There are images which the simplest of men can understand, but
which our theology has not yet fully evaluated: the tree of life, the
wreath of victory, the mysterious manna, the white stone with the
new name, the ruler's power, the star of dawn, the white robe for
the everlasting banquet, the name which Christ acknowledges
before his Father and his angels, the pillar in the temple of God,
sitting on the throne of God. The churches are still in a state of need
and oppression. Christ says to them: Persist! You will find
fulfilment beyond your expectations! If a theologian were to be
found who could fully interpret these images so as to enlighten our
understanding of faith, he could be 'the' theologian of the future.

Paul says: ' . . . I reckon that the sufferings we now endure bear
no comparison with the splendour, as yet unrevealed, which is in
store for us. For the created universe waits with eager expectation
for God's sons to be revealed. It was made the victim of frustration,
not by its own choice, but because of him who made it so; yet
always there was hope, because the universe itself is to be freed
from the shackles of mortality and enter upon the liberty and
splendour of the children of God. Up to the present, we know, the

whole created universe groans in all its parts as if in the pangs of childbirth. Not only so, but even we, to whom the Spirit is given as first fruits of the harvest to come, are groaning inwardly while we wait for God to make us his sons and set our whole body free' (Rom 8.18–23).

Romano Guardini says of the state of fulness and completion, that the Spirit effects the transformation, the inwardness in openness. Here on earth we talk of inside, in the soul, in the heart; and of 'outside', events, space, and so on. This distinction is taken up into a new unity. Hence the things, the trees, the animals, the sea, the stars, the world, will not stay outside; they will be inside a space of the heart which (without the creation ceasing to be the creation, or God ceasing to be God) will enclose everything in a unity that we earthly creatures cannot yet picture or conceive in any wholly accurate way.

But we shall be able to conceive it, with that 'mind of Christ' of which we shall partake, as the apostle promises. The heart of the God-man will be the space in which everything is. That heart which formerly had to live in such frightful loneliness, recognized by no one, 'forsaken' even by the Father, will have conquered. Everything that is will be in him. And that inwardness will penetrate everything and become open. Everything will be open. There will no longer be any within and without, but only presence. The presence of love, of love as the condition of creation, the bliss of inwardness and openness – that is paradise.

The Book of Revelation ends with the words: 'I, Jesus, have sent my angel to you with this testimony for the churches. I am the scion and offspring of David, the bright star of dawn . . . He who gives this testimony, speaks: "Yes, I am coming soon!" Amen. Come, Lord Jesus!' (Rev 22.16–20).

Note that the whole creation will be taken up into the space of the heart of Christ. There is no 'lesser' being left in heaven. All are in the presence of God: '. . . a vast throng, which no one could count, from every nation, of all tribes, and peoples, and languages, standing in front of the throne and before the Lamb. They were robed in white and had palms in their hands, and they shouted

Take us all into a
God-transparent world

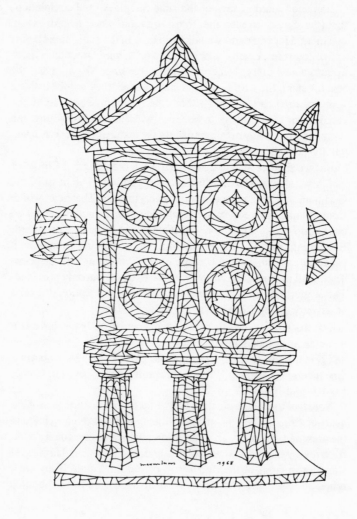

together: "Victory to our God who sits on the throne, and to the Lamb!" And all the angels stood round the throne and the elders and the four living creatures, and they fell on their faces before the throne and worshipped God' (Rev 7.9–11).

Angels and men are now joined together in worship. Augustine emphasizes that there will not be two communities, one consisting of men and the other of angels, but only one, for the one bliss of them all is to cleave to the one God. Jesus himself put the resurrected men among the angels: 'At the resurrection men and women . . . are like angels in heaven' (Mt 22.30). And Luke says: 'They are like angels; they are sons of God, because they share in the resurrection' (Lk 20.36).

Hence it is wholly appropriate that in the introduction to the *Sanctus* in the Jacobite liturgy, we should read: '. . . who is praised by the heavens and the heavens of heavens and their entire power, son and moon and the entire choir of stars, earth and sea and all that is in them and the heavenly Jerusalem, all those assembled for the feast, the church of the first-born, who are entered in heaven as citizens thereof, the spirits of the just, and of prophets, the souls of the martyrs and apostles, the angels and archangels'.

In the liturgy of the Church it is always the whole cosmos which takes part in the worship of God. The angelic hymn is never absent from worship. Human existence is transcended in it and joins with the praise offered by the angels. We must also remember that one of the essential characteristics of a monk – in the original sense of the word – was his imitation of the existence of the angels, and his practice of an 'angelic liturgy'. Of course that 'imitation' did not mean that he himself would become an angel in this earthly life, but that he was already practising for the time when he would celebrate the 'cosmic liturgy' in heaven together with the angels.

I believe that we should all practise this co-operation with the angels. They already understand us. We can and should show them everything so that they store it up and preserve it for eternity.

We are already strangely related, even acquainted, with the angels during our earthly lives. Once we attain to their company, to heaven, to the space of the heart of Christ, we shall no longer ask:

'Who are you?' We shall probably call out in final recognition: 'So it was you all the time!'

Much more could be said about the angels. But each man has his own way of setting down his thoughts and perceptions. In the creative imagination of a poet they would probably turn into lyrical creatures. A symbolist poet might see them as images of majestic things and truths. A metaphysical philosopher or theologian might understand them as personifications of ideas of the highest category. Some mystics would perhaps turn them into demi-gods.

I have tried to avoid all such flights of fancy. I have spoken of those beings about whom Scripture tells us and who are part of the life of the Church. I would never wish to 'demythologize' or 'dissolve' their reality. I see angels in the simple yet profound sense of those who serve the saving Kingdom of God, the coming of the new heaven and the new earth, the arrival of a new universe, which can only be realized in and through Jesus Christ.

Afterword

Here I want neither to summarize what I have said nor to offer a new viewpoint, but merely to remind you of something that I think is very important.

In my 'Attempt at a defence' I tried to show that God, because he is infinite, holds an infinitely large number of mysteries. In other words, the infinite God is our only mystery. He has already revealed so much to us of his infinitely numerous mysteries that even with our weak powers we can get to heaven. He has revealed no less – and no more.

I refer to this again because I know from experience how liberating that knowledge can be and yet how seldom it is imparted. Some people think they have already fully comprehended God, and learnt all his secrets. But as far as I'm concerned, a God like that, one whom you can so to speak carry around with you as a secure 'resort' in your life, one whom you can so to speak clap on the shoulder, and about whom you know everything, doesn't exist. If the real God, in all his inconceivability and mysteriousness, in the way in which he really has charge of our destiny, by suffering and death, destroys that false image of God, then the real God will not disappear from our lives. All that goes is an idol that we have manufactured for our own use.

We must see God's mysteries in our Lord Jesus. As God, he certainly knew about the mysteries of God; as man he had to attain to them. Christ's knowledge was 'already there' and 'not yet there' at the same time. For two thousand years theologians have been discussing how that could happen in one and the same person. But Christ *is* the way, the truth and the life for us, even for theologians. Theology is not only a matter of reasoning, but before everything else a 'matter of prayer'. It is a matter of reason and prayer. Both are needed for a balanced theology. And a balanced theology gives us knowledge about God which keeps to what God wanted to reveal to us from his infinite mysteries; knowledge which is self-effacing enough to say in the end: God is greater than our own hearts can realize!